THE CHRISTMAS VARIATIONS

CONTENTS

— PIANO LEVEL —
LATE INTERMEDIATE/
EARLY ADVANCED

ISBN 978-1-4803-8641-9

HAL•LEONARD®
CORPORATION

7777 W. BLUEMOUND RD. P.O. BOX 13819 MILWAUKEE, WI 53213

In Australia Contact:
Hal Leonard Australia Pty. Ltd.
4 Lentara Court
Cheltenham, Victoria, 3192 Australia
Email: ausadmin@halleonard.com.au

Visit Hal Leonard Online at
www.halleonard.com

Visit Phillip at
www.phillipkeveren.com

PREFACE

This project was initiated in 2009 when the Nashville area teachers asked me to conduct their piano ensemble extravaganza, Pianorama. "We Wish You a Merry Christmas" was written as a finale. At that time, I thought that "someday" I'd flesh this one duet into a full collection, and finally – five years later – here it is!

So, string the lights, warm up the eggnog, and find a duet partner. May your Christmas season be a merry one.

Sincerely,

Phillip Keveren

BIOGRAPHY

Phillip Keveren, a multi-talented keyboard artist and composer, has composed original works in a variety of genres from piano solo to symphonic orchestra. Mr. Keveren gives frequent concerts and workshops for teachers and their students in the United States, Canada, Europe, and Asia. Mr. Keveren holds a B.M. in composition from California State University Northridge and a M.M. in composition from the University of Southern California.

ANGELS WE HAVE HEARD ON HIGH

Traditional French Carol
Arranged by Phillip Keveren

DING DONG! MERRILY ON HIGH!

French Carol
Arranged by Phillip Keveren

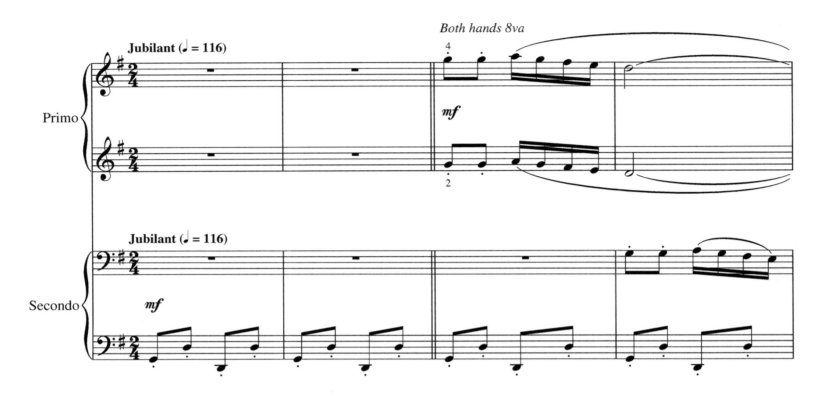

I SAW THREE SHIPS

Traditional English Carol
Arranged by Phillip Keveren

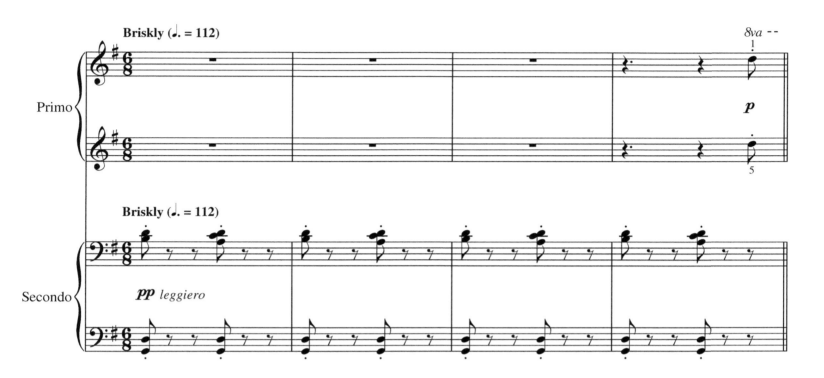

GOD REST YE MERRY, GENTLEMEN

19th Century English Carol
Arranged by Phillip Keveren

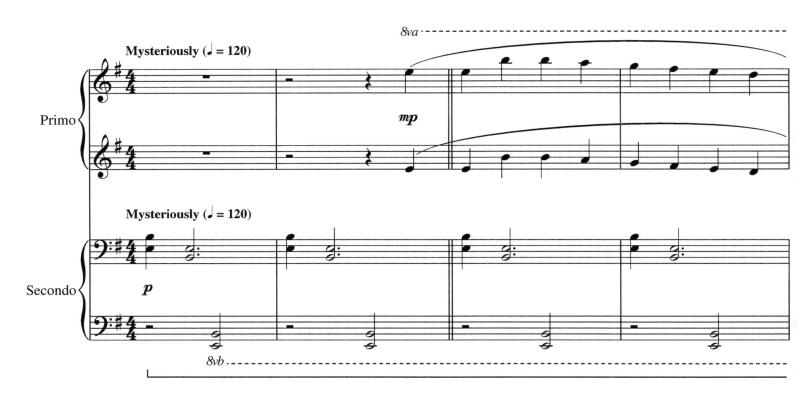

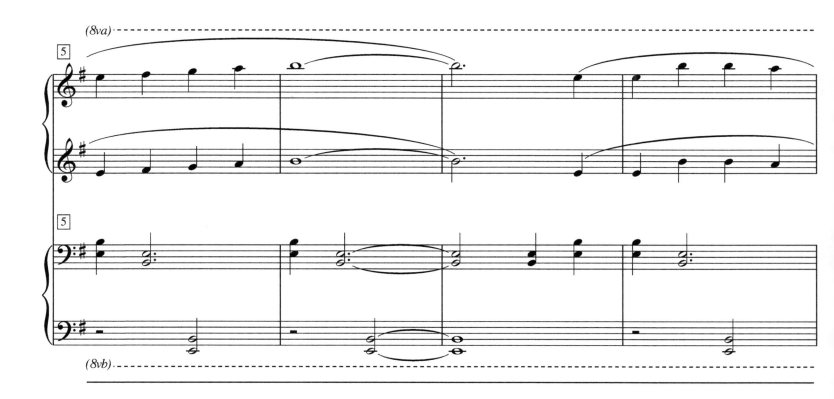

JOY TO THE WORLD

Words by ISAAC WATTS
Music by GEORGE FRIDERIC HANDEL
Adapted by Lowell Mason
Arranged by Phillip Keveren

LO, HOW A ROSE E'ER BLOOMING

15th Century German Carol
Music from *Alte Catholische Geistliche Kirchengesang*
Arranged by Phillip Keveren

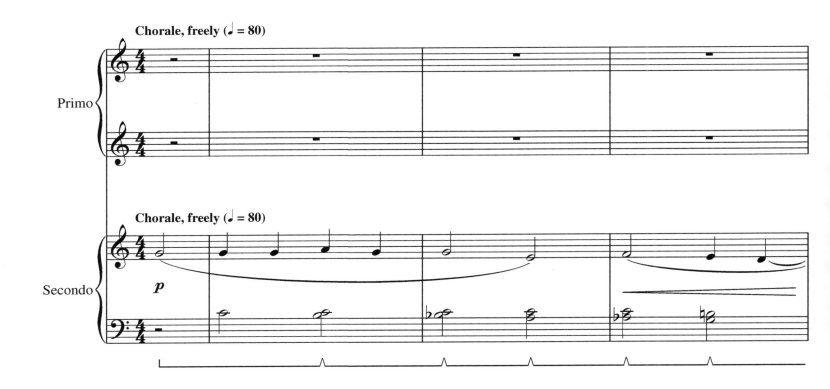

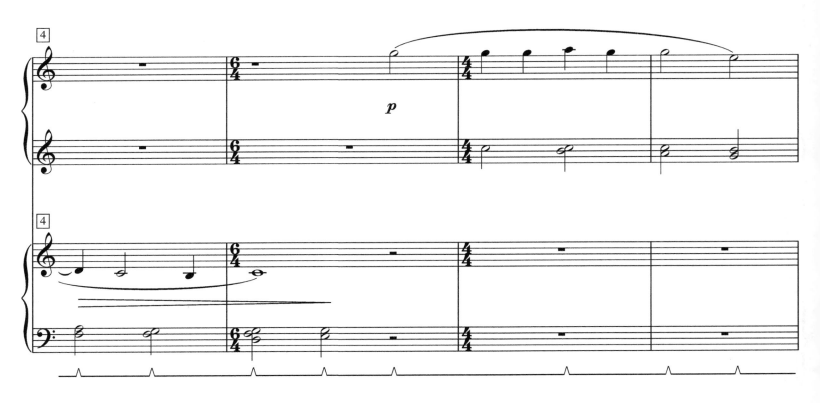

STILL, STILL, STILL

Salzburg Melody, c. 1819
Arranged by Phillip Keveren

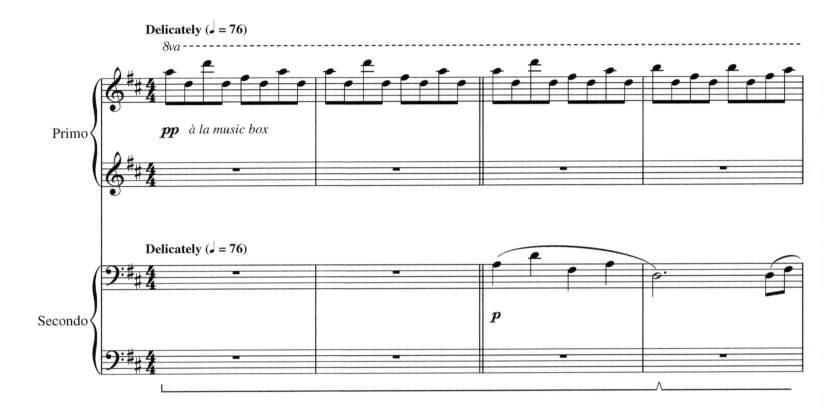

WE WISH YOU A MERRY CHRISTMAS

Traditional English Folksong
Arranged by Phillip Keveren

CHRISTMAS COLLECTIONS
FROM HAL LEONARD
ALL BOOKS ARRANGED FOR PIANO, VOICE & GUITAR

THE BEST CHRISTMAS SONGS EVER
69 all-time favorites: Auld Lang Syne • Coventry Carol • Frosty the Snow Man • Happy Holiday • It Came Upon the Midnight Clear • O Holy Night • Rudolph the Red-Nosed Reindeer • Silver Bells • What Child Is This? • and many more.
00359130 ....$29.99

THE BIG BOOK OF CHRISTMAS SONGS
Over 120 all-time favorites and hard-to-find classics: As Each Happy Christmas • The Boar's Head Carol • Carol of the Bells • Deck the Halls • The Friendly Beasts • God Rest Ye Merry Gentlemen • Joy to the World • Masters in This Hall • O Holy Night • Story of the Shepherd • and more.
00311520 ....$22.99

CHRISTMAS SONGS – BUDGET BOOKS
100 holiday favorites: All I Want for Christmas Is You • Christmas Time Is Here • Feliz Navidad • Grandma Got Run Over by a Reindeer • I'll Be Home for Christmas • Last Christmas • O Holy Night • Please Come Home for Christmas • Rockin' Around the Christmas Tree • We Need a Little Christmas • What Child Is This? • and more.
00310887 ....$14.99

CHRISTMAS MOVIE SONGS
34 holiday hits from the big screen: All I Want for Christmas Is You • Believe • Christmas Vacation • Do You Want to Build a Snowman? • Frosty the Snow Man • Have Yourself a Merry Little Christmas • It's Beginning to Look like Christmas • Mele Kalikimaka • Rudolph the Red-Nosed Reindeer • Silver Bells • White Christmas • You're a Mean One, Mr. Grinch • and more.
00146961 ....$19.99

CHRISTMAS PIANO SONGS FOR DUMMIES®
56 favorites: Auld Lang Syne • Away in a Manger • Blue Christmas • The Christmas Song • Deck the Hall • I'll Be Home for Christmas • Jingle Bells • Joy to the World • My Favorite Things • Silent Night • more!
00311387 ....$19.95

CHRISTMAS POP STANDARDS
22 contemporary holiday hits, including: All I Want for Christmas Is You • Christmas Time Is Here • Little Saint Nick • Mary, Did You Know? • Merry Christmas, Darling • Santa Baby • Underneath the Tree • Where Are You Christmas? • and more.
00348998 ....$14.99

CHRISTMAS SING-ALONG
40 seasonal favorites: Away in a Manger • Christmas Time Is Here • Feliz Navidad • Happy Holiday • Jingle Bells • Mary, Did You Know? • O Come, All Ye Faithful • Rudolph the Red-Nosed Reindeer • Silent Night • White Christmas • and more. Includes online sing-along backing tracks.
00278176 Book/Online Audio $24.99

CHRISTMAS SONGS FOR KIDS
28 favorite songs of the season, including: Away in a Manger • Do You Want to Build a Snowman? • Here Comes Santa Claus (Right down Santa Claus Lane) • Mele Kalikimaka • Rudolph the Red-Nosed Reindeer • Santa Claus Is Comin' to Town • Silent Night • Somewhere in My Memory • and many more.
00311571 ....$12.99

100 CHRISTMAS CAROLS
Includes: Away in a Manger • Bring a Torch, Jeannette, Isabella • Coventry Carol • Deck the Hall • The First Noel • Go, Tell It on the Mountain • I Heard the Bells on Christmas Day • Joy to the World • O Come, All Ye Faithful (Adeste Fideles) • Silent Night • Sing We Now of Christmas • and more.
00310897 ....$19.99

100 MOST BEAUTIFUL CHRISTMAS SONGS
Includes: Angels We Have Heard on High • Baby, It's Cold Outside • Christmas Time Is Here • Do You Hear What I Hear • Grown-Up Christmas List • Happy Xmas (War Is Over) • I'll Be Home for Christmas • The Little Drummer Boy • Mary, Did You Know? • O Holy Night • White Christmas • Winter Wonderland • and more.
00237285 ....$24.99

POPULAR CHRISTMAS SHEET MUSIC: 1980-2017
40 recent seasonal favorites: All I Want for Christmas Is You • Because It's Christmas (For All the Children) • Breath of Heaven (Mary's Song) • Christmas Lights • The Christmas Shoes • The Gift • Grown-Up Christmas List • Last Christmas • Santa Tell Me • Snowman • Where Are You Christmas? • Wrapped in Red • and more.
00278089 ....$17.99

A SENTIMENTAL CHRISTMAS BOOK
27 beloved Christmas favorites, including: The Christmas Shoes • The Christmas Song (Chestnuts Roasting on an Open Fire) • Christmas Time Is Here • Grown-Up Christmas List • Have Yourself a Merry Little Christmas • I'll Be Home for Christmas • Somewhere in My Memory • Where Are You Christmas? • and more.
00236830 ....$14.99

ULTIMATE CHRISTMAS
100 seasonal favorites: Auld Lang Syne • Bring a Torch, Jeannette, Isabella • Carol of the Bells • The Chipmunk Song • Christmas Time Is Here • The First Noel • Frosty the Snow Man • Gesù Bambino • Happy Holiday • Happy Xmas (War Is Over) • Jingle-Bell Rock • Pretty Paper • Silver Bells • Suzy Snowflake • and more.
00361399 ....$24.99

A VERY MERRY CHRISTMAS
39 familiar favorites: Blue Christmas • Feliz Navidad • Happy Xmas (War Is Over) • I'll Be Home for Christmas • Jingle-Bell Rock • Please Come Home for Christmas • Rockin' Around the Christmas Tree • Santa, Bring My Baby Back (To Me) • Sleigh Ride • White Christmas • and more.
00310536 ....$14.99

Complete contents listings available online at www.halleonard.com

Piano Recital Showcase

"What should my students play for the recital?" This series provides easy answers to this common question. For these winning collections, we've carefully selected some of the most popular and effective pieces from the **Hal Leonard Student Library** – from early-elementary to late-intermediate levels. You'll love the variety of musical styles found in each book.

PIANO RECITAL SHOWCASE PRE-STAFF
Pre-Staff Early Elementary Level
8 solos: Bumper Cars • Cherokee Lullaby • Fire Dance • The Hungry Spider • On a Magic Carpet • One, Two, Three • Pickled Pepper Polka • Pumpkin Song.
00296784 ....$7.99

BOOK 1
Elementary Level
12 solos: B.B.'s Boogie • In My Dreams • Japanese Garden • Jazz Jig • Joyful Bells • Lost Treasure • Monster March • Ocean Breezes • Party Cat Parade • Rainy Day Play • Sledding Fun • Veggie Song.
00296749 ....$8.99

BOOK 2
Late-Elementary Level
12 solos: Angelfish Arabesque • The Brontosaurus Bop • From the Land of Make-Believe • Ghosts of a Sunken Pirate Ship • The Happy Walrus • Harvest Dance • Hummingbird (L'oiseau-mouche) • Little Bird • Quick Spin in a Fast Car • Shifty-Eyed Blues • The Snake Charmer • Soft Shoe Shuffle.
00296748 ....$8.99

BOOK 3
Intermediate Level
10 solos: Castilian Dreamer • Dreaming Song • Jump Around Rag • Little Mazurka • Meaghan's Melody • Mountain Splendor • Seaside Stride • Snap to It! • Too Cool to Fool • Wizard's Wish.
00296747 ....$8.99

BOOK 4
Late-Intermediate Level
8 solos: Berceuse for Janey • Cafe Waltz • Forever in My Heart • Indigo Bay • Salsa Picante • Sassy Samba • Skater's Dream • Twilight on the Lake.
00296746 ....$8.99

CHRISTMAS EVE SOLOS
Intermediate Level
Composed for the intermediate level student, these pieces provide fresh and substantial repertoire for students not quite ready for advanced piano literature. Includes: Auld Lang Syne • Bring a Torch, Jeannette, Isabella • Coventry Carol • O Little Town of Bethlehem • Silent Night • We Wish You a Merry Christmas • and more.
00296877...$8.99

DUET FAVORITES
Intermediate Level
Five original duets for one piano, four hands from top composers Phillip Keveren, Eugénie Rocherolle, Sondra Clark and Wendy Stevens. Includes: Angel Falls • Crescent City Connection • Prime Time • A Wind of Promise • Yearning.
00296898...$9.99

FESTIVAL FAVORITES, BOOK 1
10 OUTSTANDING NFMC SELECTED SOLOS
Late Elementary/Early Intermediate Level
Proven piano solos fill this compilation of selected gems chosen for various National Federation of Music Clubs (NFMC) Junior Festival lists. Titles: Candlelight Prelude • Crazy Man's Blues • I've Gotta Toccata • Pagoda Bells • Tarantella • Toccata Festivo • Tonnerre sur les plaines (Thunder on the Plains) • Twister • Way Cool! • Wild Robot.
00118198...$10.99

FESTIVAL FAVORITES, BOOK 2
10 OUTSTANDING NFMC SELECTED SOLOS
Intermediate/Late Intermediate Level
Book 2 features: Barcarolle Impromptu • Cathedral Echoes (Harp Song) • Dance of the Trolls • Jasmine in the Mist • Jesters • Maestro, There's a Fly in My Waltz • Mother Earth, Sister Moon • Northwoods Toccata • Sounds of the Rain • Un phare dans le brouillard (A Lighthouse in the Fog).
00118202...$10.99

FESTIVAL GEMS – BOOK 1
Elementary/Late Elementary Level
This convenient collection features 10 NFMC-selected piano solos: Brooklyn's Waltz • Chimichanga Cha-Cha • Feelin' Happy • Footprints in the Snow • Lazy Daisy • New Orleans Jamboree • PBJ Blues • Pepperoni Pizza • Sneakin' Cake • Things That Go Bump in the Night. (Note: Solos are from previous NFMC lists.)
00193548 ....$10.99

HAL•LEONARD®

Visit our website at
www.halleonard.com/hlspl
for all the newest titles in this series
and other books in the Hal Leonard
Student Piano Library.

FESTIVAL GEMS – BOOK 2
Early Intermediate/Intermediate Level
Book 2 includes: Caravan • Chatterbox • In the Groove • Jubilation! • Kokopelli (Invention in Phrygian Mode) • La marée de soir (Evening Tide) • Reverie • Time Travel • Voiliers dans le vent (Sailboats in the Wind) • Williwaw.
00193587 ....$10.99

FESTIVAL GEMS – BOOK 3
Late Intermediate/Early Advanced Level
8 more NFMC-selected piano solos, including: Cuentos Del Matador (Tales of the Matador) • Daffodil Caprice • Love Song in the Rain • Midnight Prayer • Nocturne d'Esprit • Rapsodie • Scherzo • Urban Heartbeat.
00193588 ....$10.99

RAGTIME!
Early Intermediate/Intermediate Level
8 original rags from Bill Boyd, Phillip Keveren, Carol Klose, Jennifer Linn, Mona Rejino, Christos Tsitsaros and Jennifer & Mike Watts are featured in this solo piano collection. Includes: Butterfly Rag • Carnival Rag • Jump Around Rag • Nashville Rag • Ragtime Blue • St. Louis Rag • Swingin' Rag • Techno Rag.
00124242 ....$9.99

ROMANTIC INSPIRATIONS
Early Advanced Level
From "Arabesque" to "Nocturne" to "Rapsodie," the inspired pieces in this collection are a perfect choice for students who want to play beautiful, expressive and impressive literature at the recital. Includes: Arabesque • Journey's End • Nocturne • Nocturne d'Esprit • Prelude No. 1 • Rapsodie • Rondo Capriccioso • Valse d'Automne.
00296813...$8.99

SUMMERTIME FUN
Elementary Level
Twelve terrific originals from favorite HLSPL composers, all at the elementary level. Songs: Accidental Wizard • Butterflies and Rainbows • Chill Out! • Down by the Lake • The Enchanted Mermaid • Gone Fishin' • The Merry Merry-Go-Round • Missing You • Pink Lemonade • Rockin' the Boat • Teeter-Totter • Wind Chimes.
00296831 ....$7.99

Prices, content, and availability subject to change without notice.

THE PHILLIP KEVEREN SERIES

HAL•LEONARD®

Search songlists, more products and place your order from your favorite music retailer at
halleonard.com

Disney characters and artwork
TM & © 2021 Disney LLC

Prices, contents, and availability subject to change without notice.

0221
158